Angels
and Other
Fall Poems
Ride Bikes

Los Ángeles
y otros poemas
de otoño
Andan en Bicicleta

Poems / Poemas Francisco X. Alarcón

Illustrations / Ilustraciones Maya Christina Gonzalez

Children's Book Press / Libros para niños
San Francisco, California

Our City

at night
it shines

from afar
it looks like

a constellation
of stars

fallen
to the ground

Nuestra ciudad

de noche
reluce

de lejos
parece ser

una constelación
de estrellas

que en la tierra
cayó

Los Angeles

**here people
come from all
over the world**

**to make
their dreams
come true**

Los Ángeles

**aquí la gente
viene de todo
el mundo**

**a hacer
sus sueños
realidad**

3

Paraíso terrenal

¡cómo me gusta
venir al mercado
con mi abuela!

oler la frescura
de la mañana
en el cilantro

perderme
entre los mangos
y las papayas

las flores
de calabaza
y las sandías

¡cúanto color
cuánto sabor
en cada rincón!

¡sí, la tierra
sigue siendo
un paraíso!

Plátanos

cada racimo
es una maravilla
natural

un espléndido
guante de
béisbol

Bananas

each bunch
is a natural
wonder

a splendid
baseball
glove

Earthly Paradise

how I enjoy
coming to *El Mercado*
with my grandma!

smelling the early
day's freshness
in the cilantro

getting lost
among mangoes
and papayas

flowery
squash buds
and watermelons

so many colors
so many flavors
everywhere!

yes, the Earth
is still
a paradise!

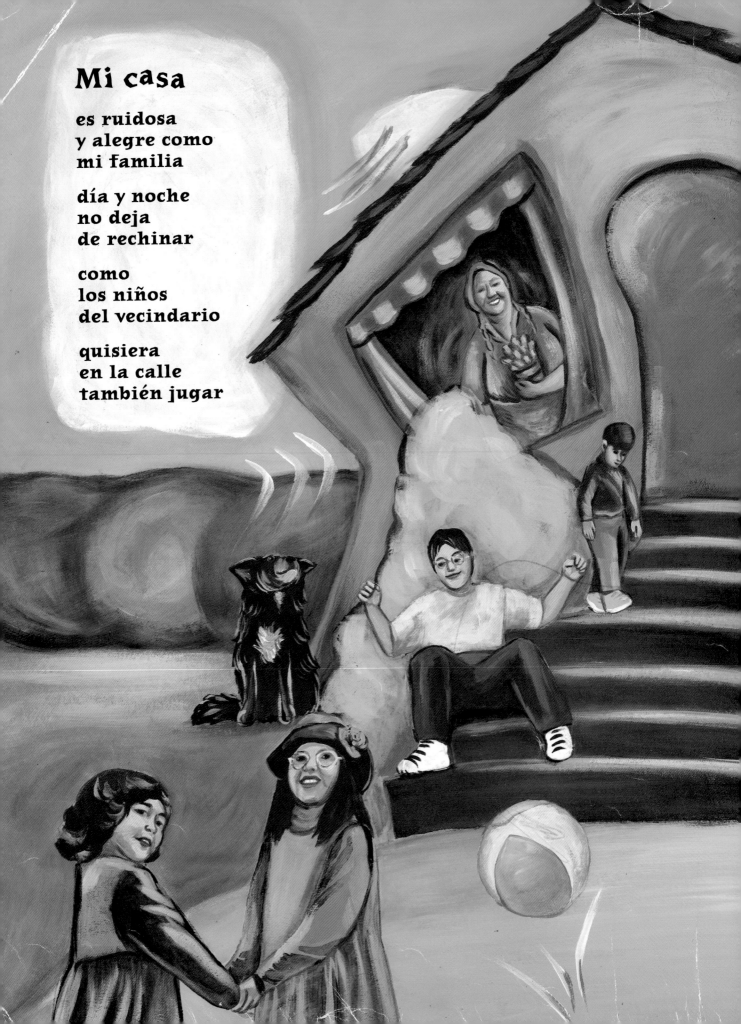

Mi casa

es ruidosa
y alegre como
mi familia

día y noche
no deja
de rechinar

como
los niños
del vecindario

quisiera
en la calle
también jugar

My House

is loud
and cheerful
like my family

day and night
keeps on
squeaking

just like
the kids from
the neighborhood

would rather
be playing
on the street

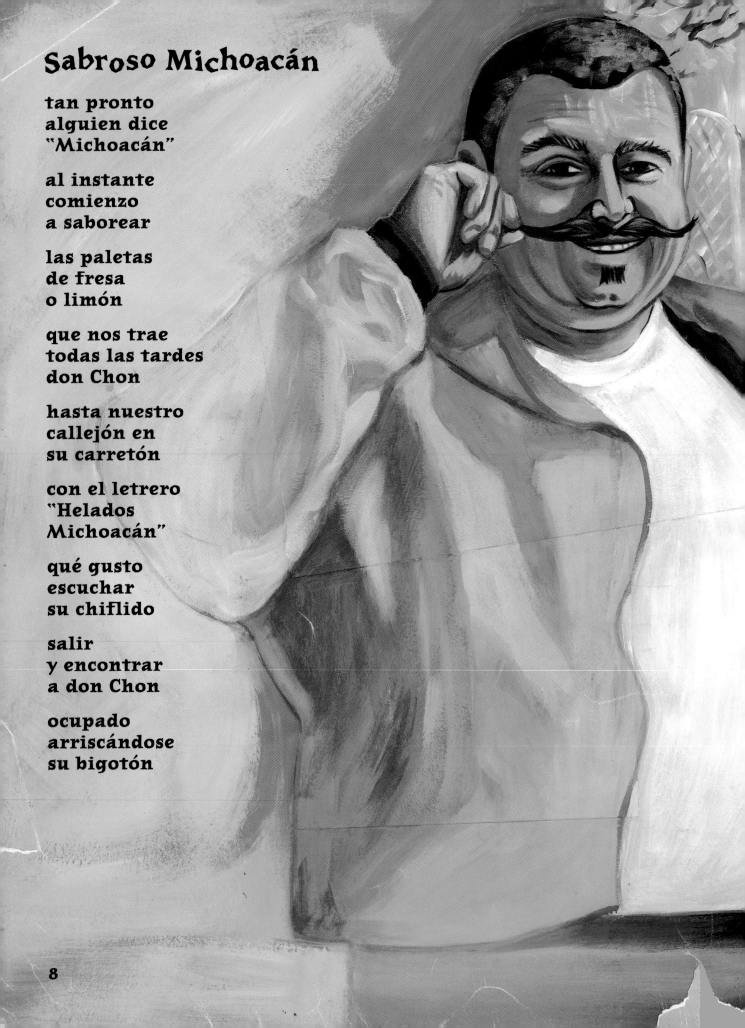

Sabroso Michoacán

tan pronto
alguien dice
"Michoacán"

al instante
comienzo
a saborear

las paletas
de fresa
o limón

que nos trae
todas las tardes
don Chon

hasta nuestro
callejón en
su carretón

con el letrero
"Helados
Michoacán"

qué gusto
escuchar
su chiflido

salir
y encontrar
a don Chon

ocupado
arriscándose
su bigotón

Tasty Michoacán

as soon as
anybody says
"Michoacán"

right away
I start
savoring

the strawberry
or lemon
popsicles

that Don Chon
brings us
every afternoon

all the way
to our alley
in his pushcart

with the sign
*"Helados
Michoacán"*

what a treat
to hear
his whistle

come out
and find
Don Chon

busy
twisting his
long mustache

Many families in Los Angeles come from *Michoacán*, a state in western Mexico.
Muchas familias en Los Ángeles vienen de *Michoacán*, un estado en el occidente de México.

My Grandma Is an Angel

I learned
Spanish from
my grandma

"*mijito*
don't cry"
she'd tell me

when
my parents
would leave

to work
at the fish
canneries

and I'd fall asleep
in her arms
once again

when she'd say
"chubby boy"
she'd laugh

with my grandma
I learned
to count clouds

to recognize
mint leaves
in flowerpots

my grandma
wore moons
on her dress

Mexico's mountains
deserts
ocean

in her eyes
her braids
her voice

I'd see them
touch them
smell them

one day
I was told
"she went far away"

but still
I feel her
next to me

whispering
in my ear:
"my little son"

Mi abuela es un ángel

el español
de mi abuela
lo aprendí

"mijito
no llores"
me decía

cuando
mis padres
salían

a trabajar
en las canerías
de pescado

y otra vez
en sus brazos
me dormía

cuando decía
"niño barrigón"
se reía

con mi abuela
aprendí
a contar nubes

a reconocer
en las macetas
la yerbabuena

mi abuela
llevaba lunas
en el vestido

la montaña
el desierto
el mar de México

en sus ojos
en sus trenzas
en su voz

yo los veía
los tocaba
los olía

un día
me dijeron
"se fue muy lejos"

pero todavía
yo la siento
conmigo

diciéndome
quedito al oído:
"mijito"

Primer día de clases

parado frente
a la *teacher*

apreté aún
más fuerte

la mano
de mi abuela

la *teacher*
se sonrió

dijo algo
en inglés

pero yo no
entendí

mi abuela
luego me dio

su bendición
y se fue

yo me quedé
hecho silla

en un mundo
muy extraño

First Day of School

standing before
the teacher

I squeezed
my grandma's

hand
even harder

the teacher
smiled

said something
in English

but I didn't
understand

my grandma
then gave me

her blessing
and left

I felt like a chair
left behind

in a very strange
world

Ángel de la Guarda

cuando más triste
y solo me sentía

queriendo llorar
en el salón

la niña sentada
al lado mío

de pronto
la mano me tomó

y con los ojos más
negros y tiernos

que he visto jamás
me dijo sin palabras:

"no te apures
no estás solo"

Guardian Angel

when I felt so sad
and all alone

wanting to cry
in the classroom

the girl seated
next to me

suddenly
held my hand

and with the darkest
and most tender eyes

I have ever seen—
told me without a word:

"don't worry
you're not alone"

Las manos de mi madre

son tan elocuentes
como los mejores libros

podan los rosales
con la misma destreza

con que antes pizcaron
lechuga en los campos

y después limpiaron
y empacaron sardinas

nada las pone más
felices que recibir

buenos reportes escolares
de nosotros sus hijos

entonces estas manos
callosas de tanto trabajar

nos abrazan y acarician
ligeras y suaves como seda

"aquí todo lo que quieran
pueden llegar a ser"

mi madre nos recuerda
repitiendo:

"¡sí se puede!
    ¡sí se puede!"

My Mother's Hands

are as eloquent
as the finest books

they prune rosebushes
with the same skill

they once picked
lettuce in the fields

and later cleaned
and packed sardines

nothing makes them
happier than getting

good report cards
from us her children

then these hands, calloused
from working so hard

embrace and caress us
light and soft as silk

"here you can become
all you want to be"

my mother reminds us
repeating:

"¡sí se puede!—
    yes, you can do it!"

La Placita

¡talán talán!

las campanas
de la iglesia
al repicar

como el corazón
de este pueblo
parecen palpitar

¡talán talán!

esta plaza a
Los Ángeles
vio nacer

todos los días
aquí días
de fiesta son

¡talán talán!

a mis hermanas
en este quiosco
les gusta zapatear

los mariachis
aquí como ángeles
suelen tocar

La Placita se localiza en el lugar de la vieja plaza del pueblo original de Los Ángeles, que fue
fundado en 1781 por familias de México, en lo que entonces era tierra que pertenecía a España.

Mariachis son grupos de músicos que tocan una forma de música tradicional del estado
de Jalisco, México.

La Placita

ding dong!

the bells
of the old
church toll

echoing
the heartbeat
of this town

ding dong!

in this plaza
Los Angeles
was born

around here
every day is
a holiday

ding dong!

my sisters
like to dance
on this bandstand

where *mariachis*
play just
like angels

La Placita ("the little plaza") is the site of the old town square of the original Los Angeles, which was founded in 1781 by families from Mexico, on what was then land belonging to Spain.

Mariachis are groups of musicians who play a form of traditional music from the state of Jalisco, Mexico.

17

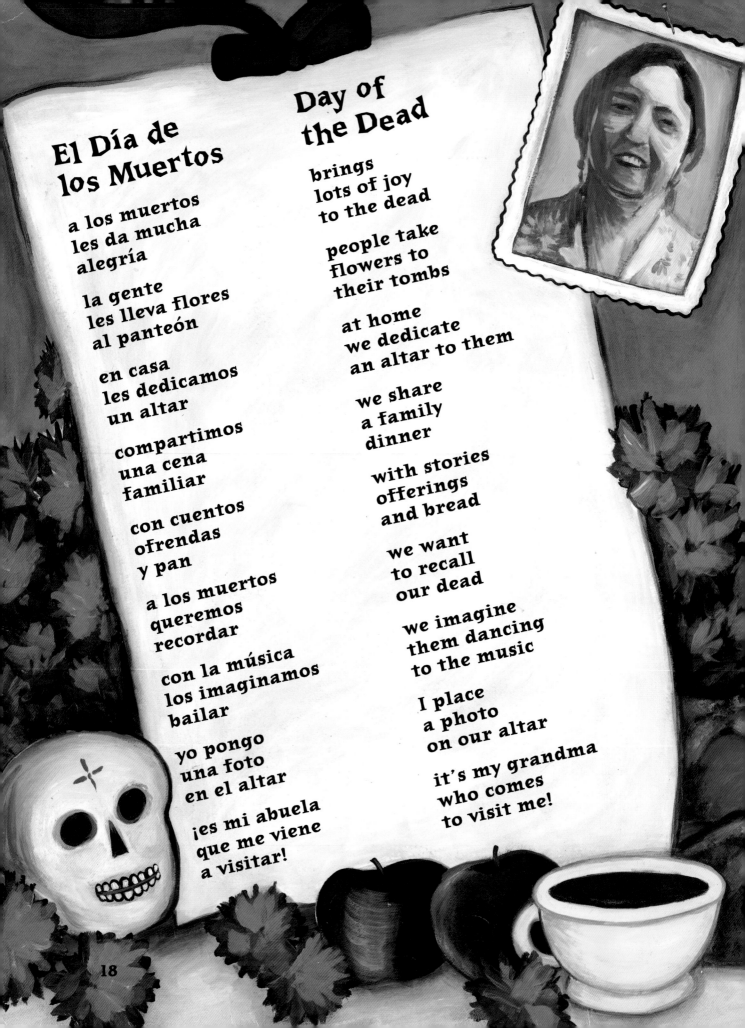

El Día de los Muertos

a los muertos
les da mucha
alegría

la gente
les lleva flores
al panteón

en casa
les dedicamos
un altar

compartimos
una cena
familiar

con cuentos
ofrendas
y pan

a los muertos
queremos
recordar

con la música
los imaginamos
bailar

yo pongo
una foto
en el altar

¡es mi abuela
que me viene
a visitar!

Day of the Dead

brings
lots of joy
to the dead

people take
flowers to
their tombs

at home
we dedicate
an altar to them

we share
a family
dinner

with stories
offerings
and bread

we want
to recall
our dead

we imagine
them dancing
to the music

I place
a photo
on our altar

it's my grandma
who comes
to visit me!

Magia dental

tengo una tía
dentista que
me hace reír

cada otoño
me sienta
en su sillón

con una varita
en la mano
me dice:

"ahora como foca
abre muy bien
la boca

vamos a ver
si se te metió
un ratón"

cada diente
luego me pasa
a examinar

para anunciar:
"nada por aquí
nada por allá"

luego de la nada
hace aparecer
un cepillo dental

¡mi tía Betty
es una dentista
fenomenal!

Tooth Magic

I have an aunt
who is a dentist—
she makes me laugh

every fall
she sits me
in her big chair

waves
a steel wand
and tells me:

"open your mouth
a great deal
like a seal

let's see
if a mouse
got inside"

after that
she examines
each of my teeth

announcing:
"nothing up here—
nothing down there"

then from nowhere
she pulls out
a toothbrush

Auntie Betty
is a wonder
of a dentist!

21

Receta familiar

siguiendo
una antigua
receta familiar

todos
nos ponemos
a cocinar mole

los chiles
a mí me toca
tostar y pelar

mi hermana
muele nueces
y chocolate

mi padre
corta en piezas
el guajolote

mi madre
la olla menea
con un cucharón

un poquito
de esto y aquello
le suele echar

cuando todos nos
sentamos a comer
mi madre nos dice:

"esta familia
es un sueño
hecho realidad"

Family Recipe

following
an old family
recipe

we all
do our part
in cooking *mole*

I roast
and peel
chili peppers

my sister
grinds walnuts
and chocolate

my father
cuts the turkey
into pieces

my mother
stirs the pot
with a big spoon

adding
a little bit
of this and that

when we all
sit down to eat
my mother tells us:

"this family
is a dream
come true"

Mole (móe-lay) is a festive Mexican dish made with turkey or chicken simmered in a sauce of chili peppers, chocolate, nuts, and spices.

Mole es un platillo mexicano festivo hecho con guajolote o pollo cocinado en una salsa de chiles, chocolate, nueces y especies.

Acción de gracias

para
los antiguos

los primeros
en esta tierra

cada día era
para dar gracias

Thanksgiving

for
the ancient ones

the first ones
in this land

every day was
for giving thanks

1. Los ángeles andan en bicicleta

nuestra maestra
Miss Baker
nos dice sombría:

"hoy no podemos
salir afuera
a jugar

hay demasiado
smog dañino
a la salud"

por una ventana
miro el aire
sucio y gris

me imagino
a los árboles
llorar

a los perros
empezar
a toser

al cielo
le suplico
una señal

1. Angels Ride Bikes

our teacher
Miss Baker
somberly tells us:

"today
we can't go
outside to play

there's too much
smog that's harmful
to our health"

from a window
I look at the dirty
gray air

I imagine
trees crying
in distress

and dogs
beginning
to cough

I beg
the heavens
for a signal

2. Los ángeles andan en bicicleta

de pronto
por dondequiera
veo bicicletas

bicicletas
en los parques
y las playas

bicicletas
por las calles
y las carreteras

veo a jueces
y plomeros
en bicicleta

a familias
enteras
en bicicleta

la ciudad
toda anda
en bicicleta

el aire es
otra vez
puro y limpio

distingo
los rascacielos
las montañas

y en una nube
veo a mi abuela
en su bici

entre los ángeles
que andan
en bicicleta

2. Angels Ride Bikes

suddenly
I see bicycles
everywhere

bicycles
in parks
and beaches

bicycles
on streets
and highways

I see judges
and plumbers
on bikes

entire
families
on bikes

the whole
city riding
on bikes

once again
the air turns
pure and clean

I can see
the skyscrapers
the mountains

and on a cloud
I see my grandma
on her bicycle

among
the angels
riding bikes

Temblor

de vez en cuando
en la California
del sur

las palmeras
por sí solas
se ponen a menear

aquí a la tierra
le gusta bailar
cha-cha-chá

Ángeles del mar

qué maravilla
ver a las ballenas
muy alto saltar

con las enormes
aletas de la cola
diciendo "adiós"

cuando al sur
se marchan
a invernar

Earthquake

from time to time
in southern
California

palm trees
begin to swing
all by themselves

here the Earth
likes to dance
cha-cha-chá

Sea Angels

what a sight
to see whales
jump up high

with their huge
tailspins waving
"good-bye"

on their way
south to pass
the winter

29

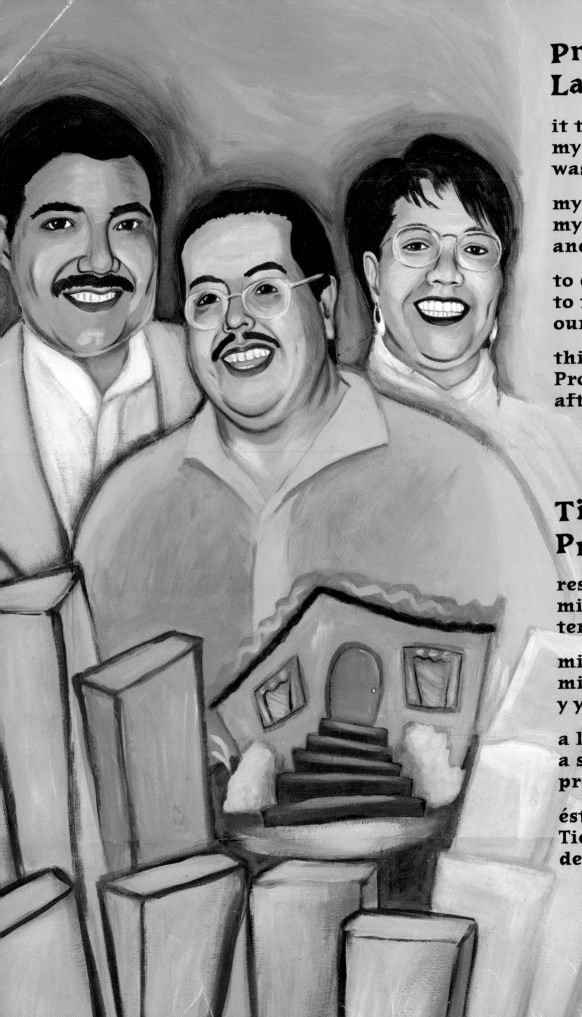

Promised Land

it turns out
my mother
was right

my brothers
my sisters
and I went on

to college
to follow
our own call

this is our
Promised Land
after all

Tierra Prometida

resulta que
mi madre
tenía razon

mis hermanos
mis hermanas
y yo fuimos

a la universidad
a seguir nuestra
propia vocación

ésta es nuestra
Tierra Prometida
después de todo

Afterword

My family has lived in Los Angeles since 1919. For me, and my four brothers and two sisters, this city is a sunny and open space where we were very happy as children. Since our parents saw education as the main route to a better life, they always encouraged us to go to college and become professionals. My brother Arturo, on the left in the picture, is an architect and artist. I'm in the middle, the poet and educator. Next to me is my sister Betty, the dentist, who appears as my aunt in the poem, "Tooth Magic." Tony, my oldest brother, is a medical doctor. Carlos is a Catholic priest. Sammy is an electrical engineer. And Esthela, the youngest, is an advertising executive.

These poems celebrate Los Angeles as a Promised Land where people from all over the world can make their dreams come true. I want to share this vision with the youngest among us: the kids in my family and children everywhere. This is the beauty and magic of poetry—it communicates across generations!

—Francisco X. Alarcón

Posdata

Mi familia ha vivido en Los Ángeles desde 1919. Para mí, mis cuatro hermanos y dos hermanas, esta ciudad es un espacio asoleado y abierto donde fuimos muy felices de niños. Debido a que nuestros padres vieron la educación como la ruta principal a una vida mejor, siempre nos animaron a asistir a la universidad y convertirnos en profesionales. Mi hermano Arturo, a la izquierda en el cuadro, es un arquitecto y artista. Yo soy el de en medio, el poeta y edu-cador. Junto a mí está mi hermana Betty, la dentista que aparece como mi tía en el poema "Magia dental". Tony, mi hermano mayor, es un doctor cirujano. Carlos es un sacerdote católico. Sammy es un ingeniero electrónico. Y Esthela, la menor, es una ejecutiva de publicidad.

Estos poemas celebran Los Ángeles como una Tierra Prometida donde gente de todo el mundo puede hacer sus sueños realidad. Esta visión la quiero compartir con los más jóvenes entre nosotros: los niños de mi familia y del mundo entero. Esto es lo bello y mágico de la poesía —¡logra comunicar a través de generaciones!

—Francisco X. Alarcón

Tony   Carlos   Sammy   Esthela

To my mother, who taught us the real meaning of "¡Sí se puede!" ("Yes, you can do it!")
A mi madre, quien nos enseñó el verdadero significado de "¡Sí se puede!" —F.X.A.

Always for you, Wendi / Siempre para tí, Wendi —M.C.G.

Francisco X. Alarcón is a renowned poet and educator. His first book of poetry for children, *Laughing Tomatoes,* received the Pura Belpré Honor Award from the American Library Association and the National Parenting Publications Gold Medal Award. He lives and teaches in Davis, California.

Maya Christina Gonzalez is a painter and graphic artist. Her exquisite artwork for Francisco X. Alarcón's poems has been praised by reviewers as "lively," "innovative," and "so bountiful it feels as if it's spilling off the pages." Gonzalez lives and plays in San Francisco, California.

Editors: Harriet Rohmer and David Schecter   Design and Production: Cathleen O'Brien
Editorial Assistant: Carolyn Winter   Thanks to the staff of Children's Book Press.

ABOUT THE ILLUSTRATIONS
After drawing my rough sketches, I photographed friends, relatives and even strangers to portray each character. I copied the photographs so that the faces would be the sizes I wanted in my final paintings. Then I glued in the enlarged copies of the photographs, and painted over them. If you look closely, you can see the outlines of the photos underneath. It was extra special to paint this book because the whole time I worked, I could see my friends and family looking back at me.

Thanks to all the fabulous creatures and folks who let me photograph them for this project, especially Myeba Midlin and Will Prater; Charlotte Davis, Alex Flores, Lisi de Haas, Becca Gonzalez, Brady Gonzalez, Brenden Gonzalez, David Gonzalez, Mary Ellen Gonzalez, Sid Gonzalez, Tammy Gonzalez, Sylvia Jimenez, Michael Lango, Nat Last, Lynne Lee, Mey Lee, Laura McWade, Connor O'Leary, Ryan O'Leary, Serge Prater, Wendi Raw, Mary Schmidt, Roni Simone, Theo Steffen, Michele Trudu; and Bow Noodles, Chives, Maui, Mona Bona Elvis, and Russel.   —*Maya Christina Gonzalez*

Distributed to the book trade by Publishers Group West
Distributed to schools and libraries by the publisher

Library of Congress Cataloging-in-Publication Data
Alarcón, Francisco X., 1954-
        Angels ride bikes and other fall poems: poems / Francisco X. Alarcón; illustrations, Maya Christina Gonzalez = Los Ángeles andan en bicicleta y otros poemas de otoño: poemas / Francisco X. Alarcón; ilustraciones, Maya Christina Gonzalez.
        p.   cm.
Summary: A bilingual collection of poems in which the renowned Mexican American poet revisits and celebrates his childhood memories of fall in the city and growing up in Los Angeles.   ISBN 0-89239-160-X
        1. Mexican American families–California–Los Angeles–Juvenile poetry. 2. Children's poetry, American–Translations into Spanish. 3. Children's poetry, Hispanic American (Spanish)–Translations into English. 4. Family–California–Los Angeles–Juvenile poetry. 5. Los Angeles (Calif.)–Juvenile poetry. 6. Children's poetry, American. 7. Autumn–Juvenile poetry. I. Gonzalez, Maya Christina. II. Title. III. Title: Los Angeles andan en bicicleta y otros poemas de otoño.
PS3551.L22A84 1999   99-10193   811'.54--dc21   CIP

Printed in Hong Kong by Marwin Productions
10   9   8   7   6   5   4   3   2   1

Children's Book Press is a nonprofit community publisher of multicultural and bilingual literature for children, supported in part by grants from the California Arts Council. Write us for a complimentary catalog: Children's Book Press, 246 First Street, Suite 101, San Francisco, CA 94105. (415) 995-2200   cbookpress@cbookpress.org

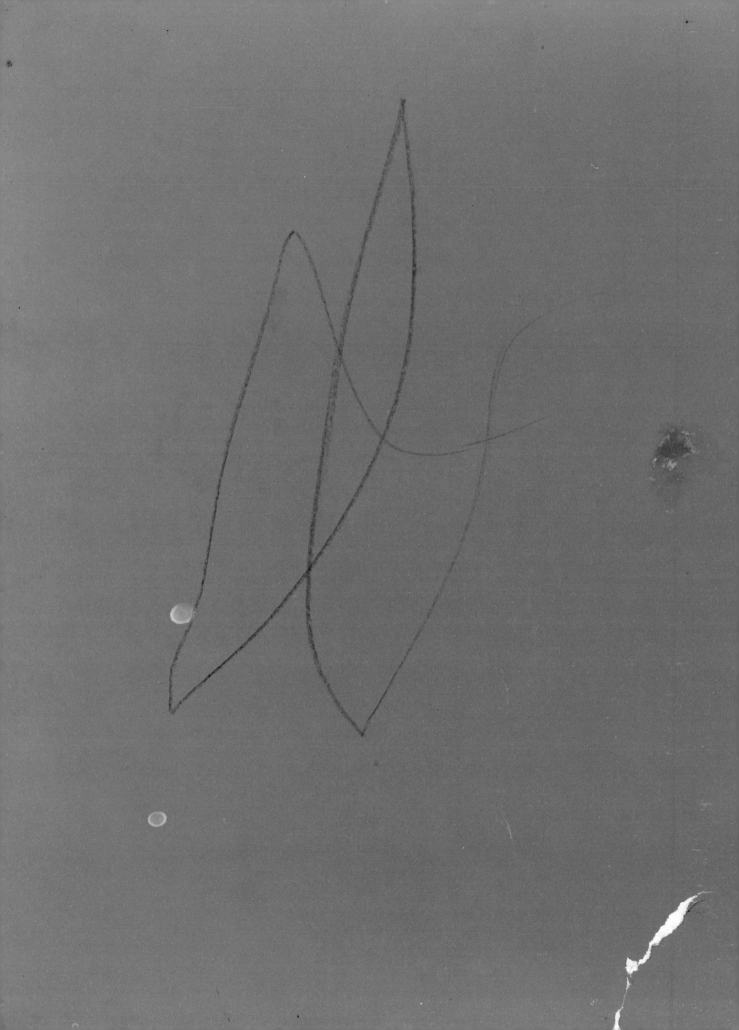